SUN

LUKE LEVI

YELLOW LEAF PRESS

forgetting my old self
I melt into the sun
and become a bird
knowing that to live
I must fly further

a spindle of shadow
behind the sunflower

some paths to the light
stretch far to reach warmth

Lightning Tree

I carry pain—
same as the
tree split by
lightning.

We are still
alive but torn
in two.
Choosing

positivity or
negativity is
never easy;
both are

appealing,
especially when
life seems
meaningless.

I like to
think the
lightning-split
tree understands

its circumstance.
It can give in easily—
let nature bury
its bones and

nourish the

flowers sprouting
about its legs.
But then the

still-standing
tree sees the sun
on its shining leaves
and the tire swing

roped on its strong arm
and the newly-planted
flowers on its soil bed
and the tombstone

placed near
its wide torso,
and it admits
its use will

continue for
eternity.
Even after death
the tree won't

be dead but
transformed,
just as the seeds
continue to move

across the land
to create
or feed life.
There is no end

to this lightning
split tree;
its life goes on.
And so will mine.

Sun

The sun
still shines
on dark days,

where not
even a finger
of the sun

pokes through
the black veil.
Those days feel

sadder than most,
but it's all in
my mind

On lost days
the sun is still
shining somewhere

on earth.
The sun doesn't
hide how things

are or what needs
to change.
The best thing

the sun does
is shine and
discovers that its

glow rises from
within,
at the core of

its being.
There was no
secret to the

smile on the
desolate days
that lacked

meaning.
The smile surged
out from

somewhere inside.
The smile
was the sun.

cotton-white cloud
soaring across the sky,
how far have you travelled?

the end of December
have I changed with the seasons
or am I evergreen?

memories return:
like the leaves blowing
against the tree trunk,
the old must be left behind
for new growth

What Is Beauty?

I have seen
beauty everywhere;
the yellow flower

sprouting from the
Texas rainbow cacti,
the choir of birds

singing in the oak trees,
the stranger helping
another stranger,

the rain racing
down the window,
the white streaks of

lightning flashing
in the darkness,
and the animal sitting

solitary watching
the sun fall over the blue hills
are all forms of beauty.

Beauty is in small things.
Fragile things, like flowers
trying not to get squashed

when the wildebeests
stampede over them,
are everywhere.

The only problem
is that busy-ness hides beauty.
Even after the day is free

you must return to what blinded
you in the first place. Seeing beauty,
for some, comes and goes.

Seeing beauty is fleeting,
as the viewer doesn't break
away from the others

in search for it. How could they?
They would have to leave
their cubicle, their office,

their building and
for a split second see the
white dandelion floating

as a spinning parachute
in the wind. It would be
a short moment, almost as if

it never happened. Beauty
opened up once that person
went outside of the busy mind

and world. There is beauty
even in storms of change.
A sailor braces for the high waves

and survives the sea.
Water pummels over the bow

and fills the ship.

The sailor survives,
knowing death was near.
The sea is respected.

The sea only obeyed the current,
and the sailor sees this
and understands her ways.

The sea can't stop
the change; she can only
embrace it.

A Reborn Soul's Ode to the Creek

There by the creek.
Water moves down
the cold stones,
bubbling up
at the seams. I
have no care or
wonder of who I was.
The breeze soars
through the leaves
of trees. I stare down
at a comfortable
blanket of moss on
a felled alder.
I look at my grave
near the creek
and wonder about
what I never saw.
I listen to finches
discuss the morning
gossip and watch
the creek near
my past home.
Water trickles down
a great waterfall
to collect in the
Columbia River.
My house had ancient
clocks that told
me of time that
doesn't exist.
There by the creek.
The light pours

down and shines
on the glassy water.
Nothing exists
but this moment.
No worries as
I float above
my past life.
No regret of my
past life above this
pile of dirt.
Wildflowers sprout
atop a hill nearby.
I stare down at a
heavy stone above
my past shell.
A line of letters
spells the name
I was given for
my last life. Animals
scurry by my grave
and drink from
the creek—the creek's
essence gladly
sharing its life.
There by the creek.
I have experienced
nothing as beautiful
as this. The waters
of life never flowed
so smooth before.
And wasn't I alive then?
The soul at last rests.
There I was,
blinded by the light

upon the creek.
And here I am,
awake at last.
I was asleep
in my past life,
but now I am alive.

The green hills
shout their songs.
Clouds stretch
in an endless
stream above
the trees, dissolving
and reforming
to no end.

sunlight
falls from
the sky

this elixir
sparks a light
in the heart

Sound of the Sea

The roaring sound of the sea
breaks into a dozen stanzas in
one quick moment. Water rushes

over broken glass and seashells
embedded in the golden sand,
where my bare feet sinks into sand

oozing up between the toes. There
is so much unwritten poetry in the
world, about us, about nature,

about other worlds. It's hard to
breathe in all of the poetry.
Poems rush by my mind like waves,

and I forget the words given to me.
The sound of the sea reaches
the sound of the earth. I am alone,

and so is the seabird soaring in
and out of misty clouds. I hear
the eternal song of the sea mixing

with the song of the land. I don't
feel so alone if I listen to the
solitary bird calling. I am one

possible answer to the call.
I am the lone bird who delights
in the natural sounds of the world.

There is no time here; it does not
exist. There is a long sound within
the seashell that's close to my ear.

A great surge of salt, green turtle
and starfish mix together near the
giant rock formations at low tide.

I turn to the rocking fishing
ship that moves in a steady rhythm
far away from shore. It, too, is part

of the music, with the bow
cutting into the waves. The
lighthouse hiding behind the ship,

with its light turned off,
braces for the impact of high tide,
where the ocean sprays upward

and glides down its walls. Even the seabirds
wait for the next note. My hand grabs
a mush of sand, then is rinsed with

the ice cold waves washing
over the beach. I only speak in
such a way when there is nothing

in my head but the natural sounds
of water and earth; their echoing
voices know no end. There are no

manmade sounds here but my breath
that is so slow it is as if I am not alive.

The sound of the sea washes away

my worries and anxiety. It cleanses me
of the rupturing sound of society.
My petty complaints

mean nothing
near the sea. I am free
until I wake from this dream.

Soaring into spring,
a black bird ascending
through clouds.
Flowing below, green hills
rolling to eternity.

Seasonal Memories

Even simple memories
serve their purpose.
Newly sprouted summer
wildflowers. Rolling green

hills covered with millions
of maples and birches.
The crinkling of fallen
leaves on the dew-grass.

Seeing seabirds glide in
the strong current above
the Caribbean island.
Listening to the strong

gust of wind that brushes
the limbs of old trees.
The smell of rain after a
long draught in the

Chihuahuan Desert.
And even after the rain
we forget about the past
drought, as if the dry

ground and lower-leveled
lakes are a distant memory.
The memory of the
drought is forgotten.

The focus becomes on
the dead grass blowing

away with the wind
and the green blades

of grass returning,
on the bad memories
fading with the past
seasons.

The dead autumn grass
is more golden with decay.
Its rebirth begins
with a short death in life
so that beauty can live on.

The Sun, Where I Must Go

Shining down
through the leaves,
viewing the moss

on felled trees,
feeling the warmth
on my face,

I reach for the sun.
Laughing as a child
without worry,

running barefoot
on the grass that
has no thorns,

talking nonsense
about clouds that
pretend to be animals,

I play under the sun.
Jumping into
the clear river,

listening to birds speak
on high branches
above me, asking if

time could slow as
I take in the moment,
I drink fully the sun.

Lying under the sun
and watching plane
engines form clouds,

feeling the sweat
on my palms,
tasting something

sweet on my tongue,
I wait for the sun to
push the clouds away,

to see its face once more,
to see the sun,
where I must go.

two butterflies
twirling in the garden
one last dance for autumn

This Old Forest

I walked through
the curtain of moss
and saw the sun
through the mirror-like
leaves. The bones of the
forest never felt human
dross and hopefully
never will. There's magic
in its midst. Many visitors
kept steady stride, full of
the feeling of stillness,
leaving emotions aside.
This old forest knows
all about life and holds
secrets in its crown.
The bluebirds of the
forest sing in strife,
and have since life began.
The wisdom of the forest
is greater than any living
man, and neither king
nor gods know so much of life.
This forest knows from
where we began. Its secrets
are whispered through
the wind's knife.

still alive
upon waking—
another gift

Changing Seasons

The good and
bad days add
up to one year.

A year has
so many changes,
with earthquakes

and floods,
with sunny
and peaceful

and windy days.
The cold wind
makes way

for the warmth,
and the warmth
makes way for

the changing trees.
I change every day.
I am the tree that

sheds its crumbling
leaves and comes
back green.

I don't look back
at all the old leaves,
for they have

all blown away.
Even a tree
has bad months.

After the winter,
it returns in the sun
and thanks each

new day for more
leaves to spare,
for more shade to give.

I am left to myself,
becoming the person
I have always

wanted to become,
always shedding
leaves and changing

colors but never
going against
the wind.

opening the windows
the news today:
birds singing
beneath a clear sky;
life goes on

Begin Again

Hope is all
we have in a
world full of chaos.

Hope keeps
us moving,
even when hope

is a surviving
blade of grass in
a burned war field.

Stemming out
from the decay,
the blade of grass

rises from ashes.
It views the black heap,
our downfall.

The surviving grass
will choose between
two views:

all is dead or
I will begin again.

What Path?

what path?
there are
infinite roads
leading to
countless places

what places?
places without end
as nothing ends
which path to choose?
there are no

straight paths;
all paths are
meandering and wild
without meaning
these paths are

crude
jutting down
long hills
and falling
into black caves

below mountains
so many paths!
there are endless paths;
even the white
clouds behind

the jet engine
is a path

no path has
led me here
if there were a path

I made it
just as the animals
made their path
following one another
through countless

years until a thin
path is made;
so do I make
my path
where others

have refused to go
straight to a new
glorious mountain
that pulls me
forward

up to the place
where I find
new meaning
in this path
called life

in bed I rest
while wind blows hard
in the cedar valley—
a calm speaks
even through strong wind

Dandelions

Throw the past
to the high winds,
where the white

dandelions glide
in twirling white
cups up to the

clear sky,
effortlessly
swimming above

the trees,
without
looking back,

until they disappear
forever,
as all things do.

my mind flips between
opposing beliefs so much
that I forget who I was yesterday

Fishing Ship in a Storm

the waves
rising and falling
spray white foam

over the ship's deck
as killer whales
jump out of the abyss

and smile as they
dive back into
the dark water

it's a race with
this strange creature
that swims

on the surface
it's a dance
upon the water

and the pull
and cleft of each
crest as the giant

waves collide
and spray water
in the air

the lone creature
with that long
white fin in the sky

makes for calmer
waters
the mysterious

creature is a big
brother to the
killer whales

and the black
and white whales
wait to see

him again
from below
the dark surface

when the great
white fin returns
and drops his tentacles

to collect
the fish
once more

Unaware of my strangeness,
I remain myself.
Does a cat wonder what she is
or does she not even bother?

Cannon Beach

I walked at low tide
on the rock-solid
grey beach. The sun
formed white sparkles
on the ocean waves.
The red and white
lighthouse a mile from
shore was on a black island.
A blurry mirage
in the ocean's desert.
People in wetsuits
surfed on the cold waves.
I breathed the ocean air
and heard children playing
and a western gull
calling in the wind.
I didn't think of anything,
and that is how it should be.
I don't know what I felt exactly,
but it's what someone feels
when they are fully alive,
when years later they think
back on the memory
and say, "So that was living."

Emptiness of Space

The dark sky
and the white lights
rise above our eyes

while rusted street lamps
shine yellow on empty streets.
To the stars, the emptiness

between each planet
is nothing—a mere step
to another friend.

The planets speak to one
another, as
they were once one.

Old friends, like trees
that were seeds from
one ancient oak.

The stars are like the
grains of an endless desert.
There is life in emptiness,

just like the Sahara Desert
with its rare pools of water
for the camel

and gazelle and fennec fox.
If you search long enough,
there is life even in emptiness.

The stars, alive and moving
slowly to another world, say,
their voices only heard in stillness,

"You were always alive
and always will be."

Reflection

The body is the womb
before our exit from
this life. Life is many things,

just as the land takes
many different shapes.
The path to the mountain

is never-ending, but the
view is always magnificent!
If I had not stopped to reflect

on my life, I would have never
seen the green valleys
glowing under the sun,

tasted the waterfalls roaring
near my head, smelled the flowers
blooming on the hills,

felt the valley rivers
full of clear water,
breathed the air blowing

through my hair
and witnessed the pure
moment without thoughts.

So, for the entire life-long
journey, I take everything in
and thank each morning sun

against my face
and look to the sun
for all my life.

Home

The Texas Hill Country,
my childhood home,
is full of life.

As a child, I breathed
deep as the bluebird
and cardinal sang

outside my
bedroom window.
There was so much life

and beauty in the green hills.
The neighbor's rooster
woke me every morning

and I welcomed the
magnificent rooster
as my friend. His metallic

green feathers shined
under the morning sun
as he strutted on the fence;

it was almost like some
mysterious tribal dance
that keeps you watching.

Mom's garden
bloomed with every color
and attracted all kinds of life.

The smell of flowers
permeated the air.
There were always birds

singing and hummingbirds
flying and humming
to the flower bushes.

Deer roamed the yard
and the hills
and would sometimes eat

flowers from the garden.
The San Antonio skyline
was seen from the top of the hill.

The skyscrapers were misty
blue from that distance
and so were the hills beyond.

The sun rose over the
green hills in the morning—
its energy waking me—

and the starch-like leaves
of oak trees reflected
the sunlight. Each morning

the trees glowed bright
and welcomed the light once again.
There were few interruptions.

Time goes by slowly
in the hill country, yet city

life moves much too fast.

I take my time, like an
old man taking an
afternoon walk with his dog.

I listen for the singing bird
and spot the baby rabbit
huddled beneath the bushes.

The flowers of the world
are old friends from my home.
The trees, too, are good friends

that are always near.
The beautiful
and fragile things greet me

everyday, and I can do
nothing else but smile.
I see all of nature and think of home.

ABOUT THE AUTHOR

*L*uke Levi's poetry can be found in *Humana Obscura, Presence, Haiku Commentary, Failed Haiku, Cold Moon Journal, Autumn Moon Haiku Journal, Akitsu Quarterly, Tiny Seed Journal,* and elsewhere. He lives in Texas and writes often about the Texas Hill Country. You can find him on Instagram @lukelevipoet, Twitter @lukelevi6 and at lukelevi.com.

ALSO BY LUKE LEVI

So Fragile Are the Beautiful Things